Doughnut Dilemma

Margaret McAllister

Illustrated by Scoular Anderson

OXFORD
UNIVERSITY PRESS

Chapter 1

Danny MacDonald lived for football.
He played it, watched it, talked and
dreamed about it. It was his best
lesson at school and his favourite
game at break. At home he kicked a
football around the garden, and at the
park he got together with his friends
for a kickabout.

You want to know if he was any
good at football?

He wasn't brilliant, but he wasn't bad. Sometimes he was on the school under-twelves team, and sometimes he wasn't.

When he was, he pretended he was playing for Lowgate United.

Danny had the Lowgate home strip and the away strip. He also had the scarf, the pyjamas, the duvet cover, the notebook, the socks, and four walls full of posters.

His favourite poster, on his bedroom door, was a shot of Keith Connolly belting in a winner.

Keith Connolly was Lowgate's captain and their star striker. When he joined them, they shot into the Premier League. He could make stunning goals out of nothing. He could whack a ball into the net with his left foot from inside his own half.

Chapter 2

One day in January, after school,
Danny hurried through his homework.
He wanted to watch TV. Keith
Connolly was doing an interview on
the local news programme.

Danny hoped that the television
wouldn't go fuzzy or lose the sound
when Keith Connolly was talking. It
was an old set, and it did things like
that.

It buzzed and flickered a bit, but at last Keith Connolly's smiling face appeared on the screen.

'What I really like about playing for Lowgate,' he said, 'is the fans. They're the best. They always turn out for us. It's fantastic running on to the pitch to all that cheering and chanting.'

Danny wished *he* could be in that crowd at Jam Street, the Lowgate ground, but the price of a single ticket was way above anything he could afford.

There was no chance of the whole family going, or even just Danny and Gareth, his little brother.

'You won again on Saturday,' said the reporter. 'Did the team go out to celebrate?'

'We went for a meal together,' said Keith Connolly, 'but I have to be careful about what I eat, because I want to stay fit. I really love doughnuts ...'

Then the sound went fuzzy, and
Danny jumped up and thumped the
top of the set to make it come on again.

He hadn't missed much. But he had
missed something important.

Keith Connolly had been saying, '...
but I'm not allowed to eat doughnuts.'

Doughnuts are banned on my fitness programme!

Danny hadn't heard that bit. All he
heard was that Keith Connolly loved
doughnuts. And at the end of Danny's
street was a bakery. It sold the biggest,
stickiest, jammiest gooey doughnuts
ever made.

Chapter 3

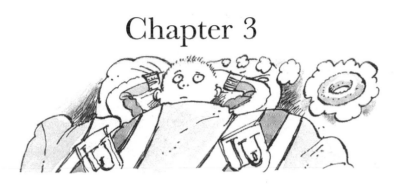

When Danny went to bed, he lay wide-awake under his Lowgate duvet, making plans. He had to find a way of getting those doughnuts to Keith Connolly.

In his house on the other side of the city, Keith Connolly was lying awake, too, under *his* Lowgate duvet. He was thinking of doughnuts. He wasn't happy.

He wished he hadn't said anything on TV about doughnuts. Now, however hard he tried, he couldn't stop thinking about them. Enormous, gooey, sticky doughnuts, oozing with strawberry jam.

But you can't be a top striker and eat doughnuts.

The team lived on chicken, fish, vegetables, pasta, and fresh fruit.

Doughnuts were made of all the things
they mustn't eat –

He groaned, pulled the duvet over his
head, and tried to sleep.

Danny knew that doughnuts had to
be eaten fresh. You can't send them in
the post. If he was going to get
doughnuts to Keith Connolly, he
would have to deliver them. He'd meet
Keith Connolly face to face!

He didn't know where Keith Connolly lived, so he couldn't take them to his house. And nobody was allowed near the team at training sessions.

He'd have to go to the ground on a match day, get to the players' dressing room, and hand them to Keith Connolly himself. He wasn't going to leave them with a security guard. He might forget about them, or scoff them with his coffee.

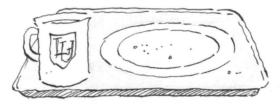

There were two problems.

Firstly, to get into the ground, he'd need a match ticket. He added it all up.

If he used his Christmas money, saved his pocket money, *and* got paid for washing the car and walking next door's Great Dane, he could raise enough for a ticket. He would also have enough for the bus fare, and the doughnuts.

The second was harder.

Getting inside the players' changing room at Jam Street was like breaking into a rock. There were security guards, and a dog that looked like its mother was a wolf and its father was a dinosaur. Danny would have to work out how to get past that lot.

There was plenty of time. It would take weeks to save the money, so Doughnut Day would be some time in March or April.

Chapter 4

Keith Connolly went to training every day, trying hard not to think about doughnuts. The more he tried, the more he thought about them.

He couldn't concentrate on training. He wondered what warm doughnuts with ice cream would be like.

The very thought made him miss an easy header.

The manager, Big Brian the Boss, noticed it. 'Twenty press-ups, Connolly!' he roared.

But he had to roar it twice, because Keith was still thinking about warm doughnuts.

The next Saturday afternoon, Danny settled down to watch the Lowgate match on television.

It was terrible. He watched helplessly as Keith Connolly missed an easy penalty, hit the post, and fell over his own feet.

Lowgate lost 3–0.

For the rest of the season, Lowgate went from bad to worse. Keith lost pace and failed to score. Every pass sailed by him.

Big Brian the Boss couldn't understand what was wrong with Keith.

He asked him time and time again, but Keith wouldn't tell.

He couldn't say, 'The truth is, Boss, I'm dying for a doughnut.' He'd feel stupid.

Doughnuts followed him into his sleep. He dreamed of scoring in the World Cup by belting a doughnut to the back of the net.

In the mornings, he drove to the Jam Street ground the long way round, so he wouldn't smell the doughnuts in the bakery.

If he saw the security guards eating doughnuts, he had to look away. Even the Boss's head, which was bald and sun-tanned and often glistening with sweat, made him think of a golden brown doughnut sprinkled with sugar.

His playing became worse and worse. Lowgate drew one week and lost the next. The fans talked about free transfers. Big Brian the Boss worried about relegation.

Everybody at Danny's school said Keith Connolly should be sold. Danny stuck by his hero. 'What he needs is a doughnut,' he thought, as he washed cars and walked the Great Dane.

Chapter 5

On the morning of 16 March, Danny was up early.

He had a ticket for the Lowgate game against Sprint United. Sprint were having a brilliant season. Danny's strip was spread out on the bed and he had bought a packet of dog chews. They might come in useful with the dog at the ground.

He was at the bakery door before it even opened.

There was no point in getting just one doughnut. He bought four, glistening, puffy, jammy doughnuts. Packets of four were on special offer. He put them in a sandwich box from the kitchen, so they didn't get squashed, and so he wouldn't have to see them all the time. They looked so good.

He was too excited to eat much at lunchtime. All he wanted was to get on the next bus to Jam Street.

He was at the front door, with the
box under his arm, when he heard a
muffled sniff. He looked round.

His little brother, Gareth, was sitting
halfway down the stairs. He didn't say
anything, but he rubbed his eyes
quickly.

'What's the matter, kid?' said Danny. But he knew.

'Want to come,' said Gareth.

Danny felt really bad. 'Look, when you're a bit older we'll go to matches together.' He wished he could take Gareth with him.

He thought of the doughnuts in the box. Four of them. Keith Connolly wouldn't want four, would he?

'How about a doughnut?' he said, and he left Gareth, jammy and a bit comforted, sitting on the stairs eating a doughnut.

Chapter 6

At the ground, Danny found his place. He had chosen a spot near to the exit, so that he could nip out at half time. He had the dog chews ready to bribe the guard dog. He'd have to dodge the security guards somehow.

The cheering and chanting began, and the stamping and waving. Danny had to stand on tiptoe to see, but he was part of it. He clapped and shouted as the teams ran on to the pitch.

Then the whistle blew and they kicked off.

After that, he thought he'd rather not watch. Keith Connolly wasn't playing. He was on the substitutes' bench.

After all his efforts, for all those weeks, he wouldn't even see Keith Connolly play. If he'd been younger, he might have cried.

'Subs' bench is the best place for Connolly,' said a man near Danny. 'They should sell him.'

'They should give him away,' said somebody else. 'Free, in a packet of cornflakes.' Everyone laughed except Danny.

Lowgate were playing two other strikers. Their names were Steve Hackett and Jim Mackay, but everyone called them Hack and Mack.

They did their best, but it wasn't working. Hack and Connolly were a good combination. Mack and Connolly were a killing combination.

But Hack and Mack together just couldn't get it right, and Sprint United were on top form.

Danny winced as the first goal rocketed into the Lowgate net. When the second one floated into the top corner, he shut his eyes. When he opened them again, Keith Connolly was slipping away down the players' tunnel.

 # Chapter 7

This was his chance. With the box of
doughnuts under his arm, Danny
bolted for the exit. He ran round the
back of the stand to the players'
changing room. He ducked behind a
dustbin. Two security guards stood
on duty at the door. Both of them
looked big enough to stop
a tank with one hand.

One was listening to a radio, and the
other was filling in the crossword in his
newspaper.

Between them lay The Dog. Call that
a dog? Even lying down, it looked half
as tall as Danny. It stared at the
dustbin, and stood up, snarling.

'Shut up, Vinny,' said one of the
guards. 'I'm listening to the match.'

Danny took a dog chew from his
pocket and dropped to his knees. He
held out the chew. He took care not to
look The Dog in the eyes.

'Good boy,' he whispered. 'Good lad, Vinny.'

Vinny was big, but he wasn't really much of a guard dog. He trotted up to Danny. Then he sniffed the chew, decided he didn't like it, and growled again.

Danny tried a chocolate flavoured one. Vinny still wasn't interested.

There were three doughnuts in the box. Keith Connolly wouldn't eat three, would he? If Danny couldn't get past this dog, he wouldn't get any at all.

Danny opened the box. Vinny sat
down with his head on one side and
his tail wagging.

When Danny put a doughnut in
front of him, he took it lovingly
between his forepaws. He settled down
to lick off the sugar.

The guards hadn't even looked up.

Danny threw his empty Coke can as
hard as he could, and as it clanged and
clattered the guards sprang to their feet.
So did Danny.

'He went that way!' he yelled,
pointing. 'And the other one went – um
– that way!'

The guards raced in opposite
directions. Danny dashed for the
changing room, and found himself in a
corridor lined with closed doors.

Just as he wondered which one to try, he heard the sound of a footie boot hitting the wall.

He opened the door quietly, just a bit, and looked in. Keith Connolly flung his second boot against the wall. Then he slumped down on the bench with his head in his hands.

For the first time, Danny felt shy. In front of him was a miserable, failed footballer. But he was still the great Keith Connolly.

'Excuse me,' he said.

Keith Connolly looked up. He didn't seem surprised to see a stranger in the dressing room. He didn't even seem to care.

'Excuse me, Mr Connolly – er, sir, – er, Keith,' he said awkwardly. 'I've brought you some doughnuts.'

Chapter 8

'*Doughnuts*! You brought me *doughnuts*!' Keith Connolly stared so wildly that Danny couldn't tell if he was furious, or just amazed.

'You said you like them,' he faltered. 'On television, you said you like them. So I've brought you some.'

Keith Connolly went on staring as if Danny were a blue, three-headed monster.

Then Keith laughed. 'For three months, I've not had a single doughnut, so I'd stay fit. Then, d'you know what the Boss said to me just now? He said he doesn't want me for next season. He's putting me on the transfer list. So it won't matter now if I eat doughnuts, will it? That's very kind of you, son. What's your name?'

'Danny.'

He opened the box. Those doughnuts looked bigger, stickier and jammier than ever. Keith Connolly gazed at them as if he'd fallen in love.

'You choose first, Danny,' he said.

'No, they're both for you,' said Danny with a great effort. He wished he'd eaten more at lunchtime. 'I'm sorry there's only two. There should be four. But I gave one to my little brother, and one to the guard dog to keep him quiet.'

Keith Connolly laughed again.

'Just as well,' he said, 'I can't eat more than one at a go. I'll eat one if you eat the other, right?'

So Danny sat down beside Keith Connolly and they each bit into a doughnut. Keith Connolly closed his eyes, and a blissful smile spread over his face.

Then neither of them said anything,
except 'Wow!' until they were licking
jam and sugar from their fingers.

Keith told Danny how much he had
longed for a doughnut. Danny told
Keith all about his family and playing
footie at school. They were still talking,
when the team came in.

Chapter 9

'Two rotten nil!' yelled Hack, banging the door.

'You're useless!' shouted Mack. 'Who's that kid, and what's the dog doing in here?'

Vinny had followed them, looking for Danny. He was hoping to get another doughnut. Danny and the dog were sent out. What Brian had to say to the team wasn't fit for them to hear.

They sat outside and Danny gave
Vinny the doughnut box to lick. Then
the team ran out for the second half.

Danny had never seen a man so
changed as Keith Connolly. He looked
on fire with energy.

'I hope they bring you on,' said
Danny. 'I'll have to get back to my
place now.'

'There's room on the bench,' said
Keith. 'You can sit by me.'

'Oh, wow!' said Danny. Then
everything started to happen.

The security guards had been racing all over the stadium. At that moment they both ran in from different directions and walloped into Mack.

Vinny thought he should do something useful. So he jumped at Hack, who was running on to the pitch, and tripped him up.

The two guards and two players lay
rolling and shouting on the ground.
Vinny trotted away and ate the
doughnut box.

'Anyone hurt?' gasped Brian the
Boss.

'I'm all right. I landed on him,' said
one guard.

'Ouch,' said the other.

'I've broken my leg,' wailed Hack.

Hack's leg wasn't broken at all, but he wasn't fit to play. Mack hobbled about and said he could manage.

'I suppose I'll just have to play you, Keith,' muttered the Boss. Keith ran onto the pitch with such a great smile, that everyone wondered what had happened to him. Danny, sitting on the bench, was the only one who knew.

Chapter 10

People still talk about the way Keith
played that day. Every touch on the
ball was a winner. The penalty kick
was magic. The run past three
defenders was stunning. And the goal
that hit the top corner stuck so fast,
they had to knock it out with the
corner flag.

Thirty seconds before the final whistle, one more impossible goal soared in from his left foot.

Keith was carried shoulder-high from the pitch.

'Where's Danny?' he shouted, as they disappeared down the tunnel. Danny ran behind them to the changing room. Then Brian the Boss appeared.

The team put Keith down. The Boss took Danny's collar in one hand and Keith's in the other as he marched them to his office.

'Now tell me,' he said. 'What's going on?'

So they told him.

'Well, if doughnuts make you play like that, you must have them,' said the Boss. 'As long as you don't eat too many. Say, two a week? I'll write it into your contract.'

'What contract? You said you were sacking me,' said Keith.

'Don't talk so daft.' The Boss glared at Keith. 'You're my star player.'

'They have to be doughnuts from the bakery near Danny's house,' said Keith, smiling.

'And I want two free season tickets, every season, for Danny and his brother. Better make it four, so they can bring their mum and dad. Or a couple of their mates. In the Director's Box, if that's what they want.'

'Is there anything else you'd like?' said the Boss.

'Yes,' said Keith. 'The Cup.'

Did they win the Cup? Of course they did.

Keith was on top form, and Danny and Gareth cheered them on. The bakery won the Doughnut of the Year Award. It has queues around the corner, every Saturday morning. But Danny and Keith don't have to queue. Their doughnuts are delivered to their homes. Keith saw to that.

By the way, after Keith scored four
goals in that match against Sprint, he
was given the match ball to keep.
And I don't need to
tell you who he
gave it to.

About the author

I never knew a thing
about football until I
had sons, but I've learned
a bit in the last few years.

I even caught World
Cup Fever, which is how I
came to write this book. Adam and Iain
advised me about the football details, and
we all became experts on doughnuts.

I called the Lowgate ground 'Jam Street'
because it made me think of doughnuts
and St James's Park in Newcastle.